Praise for The Quick and
Dirty Guide to Character
Creation

"A living story, a vibrant one, resonates with readers through vividly presented characters. Best-selling author, Diana Pharaoh Francis shares in her *The Quick and Dirty Guide to Creating Characters* how she builds believable people in a pithy, wise and funny read that could change the course of your writing life."

~James Van Pelt, *Author of The Experience Arcade and Other Stories. Nebula and Campbell award finalist and winner of the Colorado Book Award.*

THE QUICK AND DIRTY GUIDE TO CHARACTER CREATION

DIANA PHARAOH FRANCIS

BOOK VIEW CAFE

Copyright © 2024 by Diana Pharaoh Francis

Published by Book View Café in Conjunction with Lucky Foot Press

ISBN: 978-1-944756-09-3

Production team:

Cover artist and designer: Lyn Forester

Copy edit: Pat Rice

Layout and Design by Diana Pharaoh Francis

All rights reserved.

No part of this book may be reproduced in any form or by any electronic or mechanical means, including information storage and retrieval systems, without written permission from the author, except for the use of brief quotations in a book review.

Book View Café
304 S. Jones Blvd. Suite 2906
Las Vegas NV 89107
www.bookviewcafe.com

❀ Created with Vellum

BOOKS BY DIANA PHARAOH FRANCIS

FROM BOOK VIEW CAFÉ

Everyday Disasters
Putting the Fun in Funeral
Putting the Chic in Psychic
Putting the Ice in Nice

Mission: Magic
The Incubus Trap (Forthcoming)
The Elf Deception (Forthcoming)
The Giant Riot (Forthcoming)

The Path series
Path of Fate (Forthcoming)
Path of Honor (Forthcoming)
Path of Blood (Forthcoming)

The Quick and Dirty Guide to Character Creation

ALSO BY DIANA PHARAOH FRANCIS

Diamond City Magic series
Trace of Magic
Edge of Dreams
Whisper of Shadows
Shades of Memory

Shatter of Light

Crosspointe Chronicles
The Cipher
The Black Ship
The Turning Tide
The Hollow Crown

Horngate Witches series
Bitter Night
Crimson Wind
Shadow City
Blood Winter

Magicfall series
The Witchkin Murders

*For every student I've ever had,
and for every writer who is on this journey with me.*

ABOUT THIS BOOK

DEADLINE LOOMING AND YOUR characters have turned into bland pudding? Got a great idea but every word feels stale and stiff? Don't work harder, work quick and dirty!

This book is designed for the busy writer. It is stuffed with all the tools you need to quickly get those characters back on track. You can dip in and grab a useful tip or two, or you can read the whole enchilada in an hour or less.

That means you can get back to writing great characters and amazing stories as quickly as humanly possible!

I've published more than twenty novels. Trust me, I've been where you are. And I know you absolutely need this book.

So jump in! Let's fill your writerly toolbox with practical, actionable, easy-to-use tools so you can get back to making words...the quick and dirty way!

Contents

How to Use This Book	xi
1. What Do You Really Have to Know About Characters Before You Start Writing	1
2. Narrative Distance	7
3. Point of View	11
4. Voice	19
5. Appearance and Physical Habits	27
6. Perceptions	35
7. Habits, Rituals, and Doing the Things	41
8. Likes, Dislikes, and Pet Peeves	45
9. Choices and Secrets	49
10. One Last thing	55
About Diana Pharaoh Francis	57
Acknowledgements	59
About Book View Café	61
To My Readers	63

How to Use This Book

HERE'S A NO-DUH FOR YOU: A LOT OF MOVING PIECES GO into the development of a robust, engaging fictional character.

If you're reading this little booklet of mine, then you already know that and are looking for ways you can round out your characters. I'm going to talk about a variety of techniques for character development and effective ways to implement them. None of what's included here are particularly new concepts, but I'm hoping to deliver them in a way that's useful to all levels of writers.

Here is why I think this book is unique and useful. I have dozens and dozens of writing books. I have read almost none of them cover to cover. You might ask, why is that? There are multiple reasons, but the most basic one is that they are long and every lengthy chapter is packed to the gills with information.

That ought to be a good thing. You're getting a lot of bang for your buck. However, I find that I can't assimilate all that information all at once, and that I end up scanning the table of contents, and then dipping in and out, but never fully grasping the material.

The fact is I want to get in, get what I need, and get out. I want to *write*. I don't want to spend all my time thinking about how. I just want to dig into my story.

But sometimes I need a little direction or advice.

Writing books tend to be built like a machine: everything works together to make a whole, each part building on the previous, until you get to a smooth running functional apparatus.

It's a great strategy.

It doesn't work for me.

It doesn't help that I have a ton of stuff going on in my life. I know, boo hoo. Welcome to the real world, Di. It's a fact for all of us. Additionally, I have so many ideas that I don't want to waste time on reading about what other people do, I want to spend most of my time on *my* characters, *my* worlds, and *my* stories. Sound familiar?

I've taught for many years, and I've noticed that there are skills where a few pointers can have a lot of impact. In this little book, I want to deliver my experience and knowledge to you in a condensed and efficient way so that you get it, get out, and get writing.

I'm breaking some elements into small composite pieces that will help you quickly diagnose issues in your own writing, as well as allow you to see how these elements come together to make the character engine run.

I want you to be able to dip in, snatch up a useful technique, and be able to apply it right away. If it doesn't work or you want to try another, you can dip in again. If, on the other hand, you want to read it cover to cover, it shouldn't take long.

Many of these techniques you may already use, but some will be new and give you alternate approaches to character development. They may help you get out of a stall or help you to level up. If you want to report back on its usefulness, stop by my website and drop me an email. www.dianapfrancis.com.

1

What Do You Really Have to Know About Characters Before You Start Writing

You've seen character sheets, no doubt, and if not, web search 'character sheets for novel writing,' and you'll find thousands. You can buy them or find free ones. Some are short and to the point, others are lengthy with a lot of details. Nancy Kress has a terrific one in her book, *Dynamic Characters*.

Here's a secret: I don't use them.

Why not, you ask? They aren't helpful to me.

And again with the why not? Because writing down their greatest fear or flaw or where they went to school or what's their greatest loss or anything else is just too generic for me and the story I'm telling. Here are the things I want to know when I start writing. I'll fill in a whole lot of other things as I go, but these are the basics I want to know before actually wiggling my fingers over the keyboard.

1. *name/gender/sexuality* and is she single or not

2. *appearance including* how she dresses

3. *job—how does she make* money and survive? (This includes what can she afford). How does she like it?

4. *where does she live* and how is the place decorated?

5. *family? friends? what* are those relationships like?

6. *how does she handle* good and bad feelings? (i.e. what kind of attitude does she have?)

7. *how does she* handle obstacles?

8. *magical powers* (I write magic books) and how they work and what their limits or costs are (if you write non-magical books, look at her specialized skills and knowledge).

9. *idiosyncrasies/habits*—verbal and physical

10. *general personality*: happy? morose? glass half full? pessimist? hopeful? easily annoyed?

Ten things. That's it.

By filling out each of these items, you will obtain a much larger spectrum of information than you might realize. For instance, how a character dresses implies what she finds attractive, how much money she's willing to spend on clothes and hair, how important looks are, whether she prefers comfort over appearance, how she walks, and how she carries herself. Does she dress differently in public than at home, differently at work than at the grocery store? What kind of pajamas does she wear or maybe she goes commando…?

Those things also give you insight into how she might choose what food she orders at a restaurant (in case she doesn't want sauce dripping down her shirt) or if she has to wear makeup every time she leaves the house because she's sure strangers are looking at her and judging. It might tell you she likes to be fit and so carries a gym bag in her car. You might discover she wears a hat in the sun and she likes to garden, but only grows food plants and never anything just decorative.

Her relationships will tell you how much she trusts people, how much effort she puts into relationships, how close or not close she is to others, and then by extension, does she have a support system? Is she totally independent? Is she a mooch? You might learn how she gets along with her neighbors or if she smiles and greets random strangers walking down the street. Her relationships might inform how she carries herself, possibly influence the clothes she wears. They might decide where she dines at work or if she goes to restaurants alone….

Idiosyncrasies and habits are incredibly personal and what they are and how they've developed really give you insight into your character. I have a character who never uses contractions. I have another character who gambles. I have another who speaks almost in all fragments. I have another who doesn't cook and doesn't have hardly any food in her house. I have a character who breaks the rules just to break them. I have a character who is claustrophobic.

I study people, looking for distinctive mannerisms, idiosyncrasies, and habits. You should too. Watch how people do things. Pay attention to their habits. Some people need the kitchen to be sparkling clean when they go to bed. Others don't want to talk to anyone before their first cup of coffee. Some can't stand to jog over the same route every day. Some hate the squeak of Styrofoam rubbing against itself. Some never eat leftovers. Some insist on throwing anything away the moment it reaches its expiration date.

I know people who: freeze cookies and won't eat them any until they make a new batch to freeze; wear the same clothes for four or five days (except the underwear, thank fuck); take their shoes off when they get in the car it doesn't get dirty. Then there's the compulsive liar who never tells the truth and believes every lie is true, and the guy who can't stand being alone and has to get on his cell phone whenever he's alone in his car.

The little things people do help you to define and understand your characters. By giving them even just one specific habit, mannerism, quirk, or idiosyncrasy, you shape who they are so that they are individual. And of course these things will result in other defining behaviors.

THE POINT THAT I'M TRYING to make with this list is just this: traditional writing advice dictates what you need to know, and while some of those things are useful, many aren't, because they aren't specific to your story.

Case in Point

ONE PIECE OF ADVICE is to know a character's greatest fear. The problem for me is that characters are made up of a lot of fears. Which is the greatest at any given moment depends on context.

For example, if I'm bungee jumping (which, incidentally, would mean I'm possessed by demons because I will never willingly jump from a high point with a rubber band to keep me safe), my greatest fear is the bungee breaking and me dying painfully when my body pulverizes itself on the jagged rocks below. Yes, it's dramatic. I'm a writer. I imagine horrible things for a living.

If I'm worried about my kid coming home late, my greatest fear is that he's been in an accident, that he's died, that he's maimed… On the other hand, if I'm about to go on TV in front of a hundred million people, my greatest fear might be a zit. Or, if I'm finishing my dissertation, I'll be terrified a fire will destroy it, and I'll have to start all over. If I'm getting divorced, my greatest fear might be my family deciding I'm a failure or maybe it would be living alone forever.

Context matters. We all have "greatest" fears that change according to our situation.

The Take Away

YOU DON'T NEED TO KNOW all the things about your characters to get started. All you really need is enough information to make the *characters predictable in what they will do when they run into conflict*. This list of things gives me that. Maybe it will do the same for you, or maybe you will come up with your own list.

2

Narrative Distance

SIMPLY DEFINED, narrative distance is the psychic space between the reader and the character. It's important to understand that narrative distance is not fixed: it's a spectrum that the writer can slide up and down in the same story —even in the same paragraph and sentence—and it can be as remote as the arctic circle or delve intimately into the center of the character's innermost self.

I'm going to identify five points on that spectrum, but do remember that there are infinite points, and you can choose where along it feels most useful to tell your story and reveal your characters.

> The woman stood a moment on the dingy threshold and went inside the faded gray house.

This is what I call the **Stalker.** This is the most remote end of the spectrum where you only see the actions of the characters without any insight into their thoughts. Action is presented objectively with no interpretation. It's as if the action is taking place on a stage, and the reader is someone sitting in the audience merely seeing what happens. Ernest Hemingway frequently wrote from this distance.

> Cora hesitated on the cobwebbed threshold and went into the dilapidated house.

This is what I call the **Handshake**. Now you discover Cora's name. You find that she's hesitating rather than perhaps getting a charley horse that prevents her from moving or maybe getting frozen by a freeze ray. We find out that there are cobwebs, which suggests a lack of care, which is echoed by the word dilapidated. This tells us that the owner or the inhabitant of the house doesn't take care of the exterior of the house. Most importantly, we still don't see inside Cora's head. This is not presented in her voice, but the reader begins to get a sense of who she is.

> Cora hated this house and wished she could be anywhere else.

I call this point on the narrative distance continuum the **Acquaintance**. We are getting some personal information on her thoughts and feelings, but it's filtered, revealing only what she might reveal to an acquaintance she meets in the grocery line or someone she shares a bus seat with on the way to work. This is still presented from outside her head and isn't a direct insight into her mind. It's reported thought rather than direct thought.

> *Why do I make myself come here every day?* Cora asked herself.

Next we have the **Fence-sitter**. This narrative level straddles the line between outside Cora's head and inside. We have a direct thought (inside the head) and an exterior description (outside the head). The exterior is in the past tense, which also can be a marker of the fence-sitter, but that technique becomes complicated when you use present tense in the entire story. Another method in this style is to say: Cora wondered why she made herself come here every day. That version is a little more distanced because it's not her actual thought.

> Her skin prickled, her heart pounded. Sweat trickled between her breasts. *Why did she insist on torturing herself? Why bother coming every day? He didn't care. He hardly noticed.* She steeled herself. *So be it.* She reached for the door.

Finally we have the **Center of the Universe**. The reader is as close to the character as psychically possible. You could take this slightly further and make it stream of consciousness, but I prefer to use that sparingly in my writing. I find too much of it tedious to read and prefer to use it when the character is so outwardly unaware that their entire being is reduced to any given moment and the thoughts and feelings flashing through them.

One important thing you have to realize when it comes to narrative distance is that you telescope in and out, sometimes in the same sentence. You're constantly adjusting to tell the story in the way that works best. There's no point being deep in a character's mind if there's nothing particularly interesting going on there. Nobody wants to hear about how the character's bladder feels or what they need to put on their grocery list or how their heel itches or a million other inane details, unless of course those details help create the character. I would imagine if I were writing Walter Mitty's character, I'd talk about all the inane moments.

The Take Away:

KNOWING WHAT NARRATIVE DISTANCE is and what is the optimum distance for your story at any given moment is a key tool for developing characters. You can allow the reader to interpret action and facial expression, or you can dive right in and let the reader experience the moments along with the character.

3

Point of View

MANY WRITERS DON'T THINK about point of view (POV) as fundamental to characterization. I know I didn't. I didn't used to think about it much at all. The character's voice would come to me and that would be the way I told the story. Then I accidentally wrote a sequel book in third person when I narrated the first book using first person. When I went to change it to first, I got a crash course in how POV effects characterization. Now I'm going to give you the crash course.

THE FOLLOWING ARE your POV choices:

LIMITED THIRD using they/she/he pronouns and in one person's perspective at a time.

OMNISCIENT: using they/she/he pronouns and being in everybody's perspective at the same time. Also known as head-hopping and has fallen out of favor in many genres.

FIRST: using I/me pronouns and looking out from inside

one character's mind. The narrative distance is completely closed at this point.

SECOND: using you pronouns and telling the story through the reader's perspective. I'm not going to talk about second person because it's a rare method of story telling, and it doesn't apply to most writers, and I want to keep this tight.

I'M GOING TO START WITH **omniscient** because it's no longer widely used. Editors frown on it these days, though it was very commonplace in books published as late as the 1980s.

Romance writers do use omniscient in a limited way, usually by being in the minds of the lovers at the same time so the reader can vicariously experience the scenes from from both or all of the romantic leads at the same time.

Using this perspective can be incredibly satisfying as a reader because they know what's ticking away inside each character, but the characters don't know what the other is thinking. That's the definition of dramatic irony, and the reader eagerly anticipates what will happen when secrets get revealed. That anticipation creates tightening tension, which only increases the reader's eagerness to see how everything turns out.

The danger with the omniscient POV is that the narrator obviously knows everything, so why are they playing coy and revealing things in dribs and drabs instead of just telling the reader everything? The reader can start to get distrustful and annoyed with the narrative. This can be particularly frustrating in mystery novels because of course the narrator already knows who the culprit of the crime is, so why aren't they saying so?

It can also annoy readers if it isn't clear whose head they are in at any particular moment. A second ago they were inside Clay, and now they are inside Ellen, but there was no signal that told them of the shift in perspective. Skipping from mind to mind this way is called head-hopping and has become very unpopular as a general rule.

I'm going to focus on first and third person and discuss how to finesse POV to develop and establish characterization.

WHEN YOU'RE WRITING in **first person**, everything your reader experiences is through that character's perceptions and personality. Everything they touch, taste, see, smell, and hear is all colored by who they are. Turn that around and you can reveal character by how they experience the world. You can reveal fears, attitude, hopes, dreams, and a host of other qualities, personal history, and feelings.

Here's an exercise:

> *Imagine a character walking into a restaurant. So far your reader knows nothing about your character. You get five sentences plus one line of dialog to pack in all the information about that character you can. Stay in first person.*

Here's how I wrote the exercise.

I opened the door and heat battered me like a T-rex running for its life. Humid heat rushed out of the Dairy Queen, smothering me under the sticky stench of body odor, old fry oil, industrial cleanser, and mystery meat. The employees behind the counter looked like wax figures in an oven, all glistening and slumped-shouldered, sweat rolling off their skins in big, greasy drops. A sign on the register noted that the air conditioning was out, but management hoped you enjoyed your meals anyway. Management could fuck itself.

"I'll just go somewhere cooler, like Death Valley," I announced before spinning and flouncing off, my flip-flops popping against the asphalt.

CONSIDER what you know of my character based on what she experiences, thinks, and says, along with her word choices and physical behavior. We know she's female because few men flounce off. Her overall tone is cynical with a *been-there, done-that* air. She doesn't appear to be wealthy, given she's in Dairy Queen and her syntax and word choices don't have any of the polish that comes when you are educated among the elite. Nor does she sound uneducated. She's likely middle class. She's on the confrontational side—management can go fuck itself and her snarky announcement that Death Valley was cooler than Dairy Queen means she's not cowed by what strangers might thing of her. Her flip-flops tell us she's likely not on her way to or from work.

All these details set up an expectation about the character that you will continue to fill out with every interaction the reader has with her.

What she noticed about the place and the people is also telling, when you consider all her various options for details to notice. She skews negative and a bit judgmental. She sees the employees like melting wax figures, their sweat is greasy, their shoulders slumped. She's not particularly sympathetic to their plight. She doesn't say: the employees behind the counter moved with resolute patience and fortitude, ignoring the sweat slicking their skin and drenching their uniforms.

The latter description is far more sympathetic and respectful. They're not pathetic, they are patient and strong.

She doesn't look at the décor or the other customers; she fixes immediately on the employees. Think about when you go into a restaurant of any kind. Do you notice employees or the appearance of the restaurant first? Or the smell? What does it tell you about this character that she notices the people first?

The Take Away

PAY ATTENTION TO WHAT your character notices, the language in which she couches her descriptions, the tone she takes in her mind and her dialog, and what she's willing to say out loud. Those things ARE your character.

THE SAME ADVICE APPLIES to third person, but the way you approach the descriptions and voice will be colored by your choice of narrative distance, and you have the opportunity to more widely describe the situation. First person is inevitably an internally focused perspective, but third person allows the author to widen the aperture of observation.

You still remain in the character's perspective and what they see and experience. The difference lies in how you can present it. The first person tends to be (but doesn't have to be) more emotionally connected to the description, registering it more personally and viscerally. A more interior connection, if you will. There's no separation of experience and character.

Third person by definition is more distanced than first person point of view. It's still personal, and can be nearly as tightly tied to the interior of the character's experiences, but the difference is that first person gives the impression that everything the characters say, do, or think is immediate and unfiltered. The reader experiences the descriptions, speech, and internal monolog as if they are instantaneous primitive thoughts and reactions.

Third person, on the other hand, is slightly filtered at its deepest interior voice and heavily filtered at its most distanced. In terms of using third to build your character, that variety offers some different possibilities.

Here's an example:

> Laura slipped inside the room and wrinkled her nose. The place smelled of cigarette smoke, old french fries, and cloying cologne. Her glance took in the broken screen on the television, the fluff erupting from the couch cushions, the shattered glass top of the coffee table, the pictures yanked from the walls and smashed on the floor, the sound of water running in the pipes, the buzz of flies, and most telling, the dark wet stain spreading across the carpet.

In this passage, we have very little idea of what she thinks or feels. All of her interior life is subject to the reader interpreting her actions. That can be useful in a lot of situations where you want to maintain mystery or tension.

You don't have to stay completely outside her head. You

can telescope deep into her mind in the very next paragraph if you like:

> When she looked in the kitchen, Laura nearly lost her breakfast. Tremors ran through her and her stomach churned. *This can't be happening. It's not happening.* But nothing she could say would change the small slumped figure on the floor, the child's blue eyes staring vacantly. Laura swiped at the tears fogging her sight, clenching her teeth against the scream rising in her chest.

In this example, we know how Laura is feeling. We have her physical and mental reactions. We go deep into her mind, getting her physical reactions as you would in first. Paired with the more distanced paragraph before, you have a flexibility of narrative that you don't have in first and can control how the reader experiences the character from moment to moment. You can withhold the interior life to push the tension, then invite the reader inside to achieve that emotional connection that's so satisfying.

The Second Take Away

WITH FIRST PERSON POINT OF VIEW, you are inside the character's head experiencing life as they do, and experiencing everything with them as if you are in their skin. The reader knows everything as it happens. In third, you have some flexibility on when you reveal the interior life and when you withhold it, which engages the reader in psychologically analyzing the character.

4

Voice

CHARACTER VOICE IS how someone communicates who they are through speech and thought. You establish the voice through word choice, syntax, grammar, speech habits, accents, language taboos, cadence of speech, colloquialisms, what they are willing to say out loud, what they feel compelled to hide, and their tone in any given situation.

Many writers will try to capture exactly how a speaker sounds. Many readers get annoyed by this, because, again, it can be tedious to read. Now if you pick up *Of Mice and Men*, you'll see Steinbeck uses it relentlessly. If you read Zora Neale Hurston's fiction, you're going to find yourself immersed in thick colloquial speech. Interestingly, in *Their Eyes Were Watching God*, Pheoby's internal voice is educated and cultured, but her speaking voice is broken and uneducated. It was important for Hurston to write black voices accurately, but correct English of the internal voice demonstrates that her characters aren't stupid, as white people of the period often believed.

Some writers attempt to capture the accents in such a way that it makes the prose difficult to read. For instance:

"Ain't gwin down t'th' store, 'less yous agonna be payin' me." Or another example: "Ah don' lak how yer speakin' t'me, George. Ahm gonna be tellin' yo' momma." You go more phonetic and use a lot of apostrophes where letters are dropped.

You can accomplish much the same thing in both cases by *suggesting* the accent. "Ain't gonna go to the store unless you're gonna be paying me," or "I don't cotton to how you're speaking to me, George. I'm going to be talking to your momma." The first gives the impression of a less educated speech, while the second captures more of the southern cadence and syntax to give a sense of the southern accent.

The key here is that consistency and volume matter. Maintaining speech habits throughout the story is critical. Characters evolve and so do their voices, but some things must remain consistent. If you write their dialog well, the reader will know who is speaking without the help of a dialog tag.

Tools for Developing Voice

WORD CHOICE: Everybody uses a vocabulary they feel most comfortable with. They have specific habits of description, swearing, slang, and so on. There are words that I'd use that you never would and vice versa. Some words are particular to geographic areas, like pop rather than soda, tennis shoes rather than sneakers, or lightning bugs rather than fireflies. Use non-American English: boot rather than trunk or loo rather than bathroom. My mother says warsh and squwarsh and goes around conners (wash, squash, corners). Pick words that your character would use based on their background and experiences and personality.

SLANG, CURSING, AND COLLOQUIALISMS: These might be considered a subset of word choice, but worth addressing on their own. Slang, cursing, and colloquialisms can identify where a person comes from, where they've been living, and they help situate the character as a person. For instance, "bless your heart" is infamously southern, as is y'all. In my Horngate books, my Texan character uses Texan colloquialisms. My main character, Max, frequently says Holy Mother of Fuck. I know someone who "dips" when he leaves. As in, "we'll just dip after the first movie." "I'll just vibe it," means "I'll figure it out as I go along."

You can assign specific word habits to various characters to help distinguish them and reveal who they are. The main thing is to be careful not to overwhelm your reader with too much, and not to use references that are too specifically situated in time or trends, and ephemeral language that it quickly becomes dated I avoid language that is tied to flash-fads or events that significantly date the story. For instance, a reference to Kim Kardashian dating Pete Davidson would quickly become stale. By the time I publish this, you will know exactly what that means because it will be very very stale. Another example would be a word like "fleek," which was momentarily popular and now has more or less vanished out of public use.

SYNTAX: This is the order that words go in. You can play with this in a lot of subtle ways, or you can go really obvious. One of the most famous examples of playing with syntax is Yoda's speech. Instead of subject, verb, object, his syntax is object, subject, verb. Happy you are. Content I am. It sounds very strange because it's not what we are used to.

Now think about how you can shift syntax in minor ways for your characters. I have one character who never uses contractions, so his speech is very formal, even stilted. You can have a character who drops some words. Instead of: I don't want to go, your character can say: don't want to go. You can have your character repeat some words, or speak ten words when one would do. In Dicken's *Bleak House*, Mister Turveydrop gives long florid speeches that circle and double-back and say a whole lot of nothing, and at the end, he will say, "In short," and give a quick little summary of the lengthy thing he just said.

GRAMMAR: You can have your character speak in fragments or run-ons. You can have your character speak in all exclamations. Think about the rules of grammar and how you can adjust for a character's particular speech patterns. You can create misunderstandings by artfully playing with pronoun references or modifiers. The key is to know the rules of the grammar that you're messing with so it's clear you aren't making a mistake, but giving your character a speech quirk.

TABOOS: There are all kinds of words that are taboo, and many of those change according to the situation and the company you're keeping. For instance, cursing at work or at a funeral or wedding would be taboo. Saying 'Christ on a cracker' in a Christian setting could be offensive and therefore taboo. Calling women girls might be taboo. Society has rules and expectations for social behavior that includes language choices. Have your character break a few or simply not care. Suppose you've got a shy person who's known to be polite and suddenly she tells someone to mind their own business. It's taboo for her, and if it's her boss or mother-in-law, even more so.

CADENCE: This particular element is a lot harder to pin down. It involves the musical beat of the language. You might use all hard sounds in a character's dialog, or use long, multisyllabic words.

COMPARE THE FOLLOWING:

I don't like you. You're a snake. I wouldn't spit on you if you were on fire

I do not much care for you. You, sir, are a cold, soulless snake, and I would not waste my spit on you if the devil caught your britches on fire.

OBVIOUSLY THE SECOND will read more slowly, but when you speak the two sentences aloud, you can hear the slower and more even cadence in the second, whereas the first example is quick and staccato. There's also a southern drawl quality to the second and a more northern, New Yorky sort of quick, sharp punch to the first.

Paying attention to cadence allows you to reinforce personality traits to further reveal your character.

WHAT CAN BE SAID: This particular technique goes farther than the taboo. Taboo usually stems from rules that come from outside of a character. They might have been internalized in terms of manners or proper behavior, but they had to be taught and are part of getting along socially.

In this case, what can be said refers to what a character is willing to say and in front of whom. What is safe to say? What is going to make a difference? What will get you heard? What words or topics may you discuss? Obviously this is all contextual and depends upon who is listening. You would not say things to your parent that you'd say to your best friend; you would not say things to a child that you would say to an adult; you would not say things to your boss that you might say to your coworker.

What Can't Be Said: Obviously this is a correlative to what can be said. Once again, it comes down to the specifics of your character. What don't they feel safe or comfortable revealing? Most people don't want to talk about their dildo in their nightstand, for instance. Or when they were humiliated. Or have words they don't feel comfortable speaking aloud. Knowing what can't be said, and what the character will actively avoid saying is just as important as knowing what they are willing to say.

Tone: We are all familiar with tone. With being snarky, being disdainful, being mean, being dismissive, being welcoming, and so on. Obviously your choice of language will matter in determining tone. Think about all the various meanings of "dude," when said in different tones. Commiseration, surprise, saying hello, and so on. You can identify a character by giving them a general tone. Eeyore is always depressed. The glass is not only empty, there's a hole at the bottom. Meanwhile, Bugs Bunny never gets angry. His tone is always friendly, but he's aware he's taunting. Yosemite Sam blusters and is generally angry, or at the very least, short-tempered.

Compare the following:

I don't want to go.

I'm not going unless you feed me tacos and chocolate and let me nap when I want.

Fuck off. I'm staying.

Whatever. I don't want to go anyway.

No, it's fine. Really, I don't want to go. I mean, I would if you wanted me to, but it's not like I was hoping to be asked or anything.

EACH OF THOSE responses carry a variation in tone. Tone will change for every character as different situations arise. The key is to use tone to reveal your character in any particular moment.

SPEECH QUIRKS: This technique overlaps with others, but I want to single it out as a particularly powerful one. It's also easily overused and can become more caricature than character. Speech quirks are what I call habit language. Specifically, habits of speech that someone develops and can help define them. I had a teacher friend who ended almost *every* sentence in class with, "right?" It was annoying, to be honest, but as a character trait, has a lot of possibilities.

Some people use "okay" as a way to organize their thoughts and punctuate their speech with it whenever they need to pause and gather themselves. It's as if they can't stand the silence and need to fill it. I like to start sentences and paragraphs with "So." So I was thinking. So you know how to get to the store? So I slept through my alarm. I used to use 'apparently' a lot, usually to be sarcastic. "Apparently I shouldn't have picked the hot pan up without gloves."

Give your character a language quirk and see where it takes you. It can be a single word, a phrase, or maybe speaking in questions. The choices are endless.

The Take Away

There are a lot of language techniques that are effective for developing characters. Play with some to see what will help make your character's voice unique while helping to define who they are.

5

Appearance and Physical Habits

HAVE you ever heard the phrase: you are what you wear? There's a lot of truth in it. Clothes and accessories often reflect a person's personality. They can also reflect financial status, the kind of work and hobbies a person does, how vain they are, favorite colors, and even what they had for their last meal. You can stereotype people with clothes. For instance, the thug who wears the dirty white 'wife-beater' undershirt; the homosexual man wearing pink or pastel colors; the lesbian woman wearing flannel; the librarian with a tight bun and horn-rimmed glasses; the hooker in tight spandex; the southern gentleman in a white suit.

Choosing appearance—from clothing to skin issues to slouching to walking pigeon-toed to hair to facial expression—should be done to help you define and reveal your characters. For some, clothes can be a weapon. For others, clothes can be a disguise. They can be a way to intimidate or flaunt wealth. When dressing your characters, there are few things to keep in mind.

1. Why is your character wearing the clothes they are wearing? Is it for comfort? To make someone else happy? For specific tasks (work clothes or scuba diving, for instance)? To show off? To attract someone?

Identifying the purpose will allow you to connect the clothing choices to what this particular character would choose under any given circumstances. On top of that, those choices reveal how that character perceives the situation, whether they think it's important or ridiculous or potentially embarrassing. If you want to know your character better, imagine what they'd wear in several different situations.

Some suggestions: upon attending a gathering where they will be honored and have to give a speech; upon going to work out in a public place; attending a family gathering; a job interview; a high school reunion; a day at the beach; going to the grocery store.

I grew up on a cattle ranch and the local community college would bring agriculture students out when we were working cows. They'd be helping to castrate, brand, tag, worm, vaccinate, treat pink eye, and so on. It was a dirty job. You always walked away covered in cow shit, blood, pee, and a variety of other unpleasant substances. But even so, inevitably at least one woman, usually more, would wear sandals or pumps, long nails, makeup, and delicate clothing. They still had to work and they did not like it. But maybe they couldn't stop themselves from dressing up. I know someone who will not leave the house without her makeup on, not even to get the mail on the corner. It could be that these women are so deeply ingrained with the idea that they must look a certain way that they cannot adjust for the occasion. That makes for a great character quirk.

Clothes and jewelry are incredibly personal, and we choose what we wear for many reasons. Pay attention to not only what your characters wear, but why, and your characters will have far greater depth and dimension.

2. WHAT CAN YOUR CHARACTERS AFFORD? Where do they shop? How much are they willing to spend on their apparel?

Carrie, in *Sex in the City,* is infamous for having an enormous closet of expensive shoes. Some people will scrimp and eat ramen every day so they can buy designer clothing. Some will go into serious credit card debt in order to create a public image of wealth or taste or being successful. Some people only shop at thrift stores. Some can barely afford to go to Walmart. Some are going to get their clothing through charity sources. Some have small wardrobes because clothes aren't that important. Others use entire rooms as closets.

As you think about your characters and their clothing habits, you'll have to consider how they get their money, whether shopping is a social activity or possibly a coping activity. How big is their living space? How do they wash clothes or do they have to dry clean a lot of them? All those little details become part of their everyday lives and personalities. Some people have a few pieces of very expensive clothing or footwear that they are tremendously careful of because they can't afford to replace them. How will they wear them? And what sort of special occasion would be important enough to wear them?

Some clothing is sentimental, maybe belonging to a friend or loved one who is gone. Possibly something you wore at a special event and evokes great memories. Your character might have clothing that they would like to burn but keep anyway.

3. What sorts of clothing or looks do they admire but can't or don't wear for some reason? It might be skin tone or body type that prevents it, or the inability to carry the look off, or maybe feeling that they couldn't get away with wearing something like that. Or maybe they fear being judged.

4. What sort of clothing makes them feel strong and powerful? Feels like armor against whatever conflicts might be happening in their lives?

Aside from clothing, you have a number of other considerations when it comes to appearance. Hair is one. How much time does your character put into hair care? How much into styling? Is their hair high maintenance or brush and go? Do they dye their hair? Do they worry about going gray? Going bald? Receding hairline?

Moving along from the head to the rest of the body, do they shave, pluck, or wax? What about fingernails? Are they carefully painted? Fake or real? Cut short or long? Does your character get mani-pedis?

There are assumptions we all make about people's appearances that you can play into or overturn. The man who wears tailored Armani suits who isn't bothered by getting wine spilled all over him. The woman dressed in a flannel shirt and jean shorts who gets wildly upset because she found a hole in her shirt. The grandfather dressed head-to-toe in gold sequins, or the accountant who dresses in drag for work. A non-binary real estate agent who alternately wears three piece suits and dresses.

What about those who want to hide parts of their bodies? Warts or rough skin or a birthmark? Or maybe ugly feet? How many want or have had plastic surgery to straighten a nose, plump up lips, get bigger breasts, a round butt, calf muscles or something else? There are tattoos and piercings, both of which tend to be very personal and reveal a great deal about a person.

Thinking about how your character likes or dislikes their own body is incredibly useful for how you portray them and offers another avenue of insight into who they are.

LAST, I WANT TO TALK ABOUT PHYSICALITY and physical habits. Physicality is how a person moves, stands, sits, and lays. I had a friend who was a captain in the air force who ran with her hands upraised and flinging out and in as she paddled the air. I'm not sure how she didn't fall down.

My dad had a surgery that fused his neck, freezing his head in a singular position. He couldn't turn it side to side or up and down. When he sat, he looked straight ahead, and when he stood, his neck was permanently bent at an angle.

I knew a girl in high school who had larger breasts than she was comfortable with, so she carried herself hunched over with her shoulders drawn in to try to minimize them. I doubt she was aware. I know a young woman who stands hunched all the time, and when she runs, she's bent forward like she's perpetually falling.

Some people can't stand still. They have to be bouncing or fidgeting. Some people hate standing at all; they have to lean against something or sit. Some people amble, others walk like they are in a race. Some people stomp and others move gracefully. Some of us constantly trip or whack into things.

I know people who blink a lot more than seems normal. I know people who lick their lips constantly, or sniff all the time, or snore, or are always scratching at some part of themselves.

All these movements and ways of being are windows into your character. How they carry themselves at any given time tells a little bit more about them as people, but also how they are feeling in the moment. Movement can reinforce how you want the reader to perceive them.

Along with ordinary physicality comes physical habits. These are movements that people do when they are nervous or bored or upset. I remember watching an interview with a recent widower. The interviewer asked about his dead wife, and while I don't remember the answer, the man's physical behavior stuck with me. He averted his gaze and stroked his fingers over the table in short, slow strokes. He felt too much to sit still. Smoothing his fingers over the table while he responded allowed him to focus less on the feelings and the words so that he didn't break down in tears. Likewise, not looking at the interviewer allowed him some ability to stay private with his emotions.

Have you ever been sitting at a table with other people and the table vibrates or rocks because someone is shaking their foot or tapping their toes? Have you ever been irritated or bored and taken to drumming your fingers on the table? I've been known to perform finger exercises when I'm sitting through a PowerPoint presentation. It helps me not to fall asleep. Some people snap their gum when chewing, others chew their lips when nervous. Many performers swallow a lot when getting ready to go on stage or giving a presentation. I've met people suck their teeth loudly—which gives me all sorts of ideas about them that probably are all wrong, but what kind of person sucks their teeth? Have you seen someone twisting their hair around their fingers or otherwise playing with it?

Everybody at some point has some kind of repetitive physical habit, often when under some kind of stress. It's another potential insight into who your character is.

Start watching people. Look at how they dress, carry themselves, and if they have physical habits. Take notes and use them.

The Take Away

Almost all writers recognize that description is important. We don't often pause to consider exactly why. Every little detail about your character's appearance, ways of movement, and physical habits is an opportunity to show who they are. You can hint at hidden qualities that later the reader realizes they should have seen all along. It makes for a delightful reading experience when even the smallest pieces of description can reveal a character to you.

6

Perceptions

How characters interpret what their senses tell them gives you a rich opportunity to further develop them. We have five senses bombarding us with information. Our brains have to acknowledge and sort that information and assign a value to it. That value might be dangerous or disgusting or delightful or a billion other things. Did you know the smell of rotting flesh is introduced into natural gas so that if you smell it in the house, you have a visceral reaction that something is wrong? The smell would mean the gas is leaking. Without that scent, you wouldn't know and would likely die.

This process of is automatic and usually happens at a subconscious level. You, as writer, can take advantage of that process to give depth and breadth to your character.

People tend to notice what makes them unhappy first. Maybe it's a bad smell. Maybe it's an uncomfortable texture. Maybe it's a sound that drives them nuts or visual stimulants that give them a headache. Maybe it's a taste that makes them instantly want to vomit.

When I've had to prepare for a colonoscopy, the doctors have insisted on giving me a chemical to add to a flavored drink, and I'm told to drink it. Something about that chemical hits my tongue, and instantly I start to throw up. I think it's a bitterness, but honestly I'm not sure. When I was pregnant, the smell of fish would have me vomiting. A friend of mine has trypophobia, which is a fear of patterns of holes. My dad hated cilantro and said it tastes like soap. Don't get me started on his opinions on broccoli.

My point is that each one of us has individual dislikes and often those are linked to experiences in our lives (my inability to eat fish is from a bad experience), or something inherent to ourselves. We each have our own unique responses to negative stimuli.

Imagine walking into a flea market on a hot summer's day. Impressions might include: humidity and a sense of smothering because of it; the stench of body odor and frying foods; the uneven ground that makes twisting an ankle likely; the sticky slide of sweat when you brush past someone and touch their skin; the sensation of grime floating in the air and clinging to you.

On the other hand, someone else might walk into the same scene and not even smell the body odor and be so used to the humidity they don't notice it either. The frying foods might smell delicious (funnel cakes!) and since they're wearing hiking boots, the ground is just fine. They hardly care when they bump up against someone else who's sweating.

That doesn't mean they don't have negative impressions. Indeed they do. They hate the overwhelming stink of perfume. Stir in the thick stench of cigarette smoke and they can hardly breathe. A squeaking sound cuts through the crowd noise like fingernails on a blackboard. They've got a heat rash between their thighs, and it's rubbing painfully.

Who each character is dictates *what* they notice, what bothers them, what provides joy, and what scares them. The reverse of that is that you can create who they are by choosing their focus. Choose the details they notice and care about. Choose what bothers them in a scene.

The other side of the perception window is what other characters see and think. Consider the saying: you can't judge a book by its cover. We all know this, yet we do that all the time. Something doesn't look appetizing, and we don't want to eat it. Ted Bundy looked handsome and friendly and women got in his car. We see a big burly man in a hoody pulled up over his head and low slung jeans and we think danger! (Maybe that's a woman thing).

All that said, in fiction, what other characters think about each other is an excellent technique for character construction. Sometimes I conduct interviews with my characters and ask them about each other. What they answer tells me about both them and the other characters.

Here's an example from an interview I conducted with my characters. My character, Ryland, talks about Shaye:

> He's a merchant brat. A scalawag. A rogue of the basest sort. Cousin of the Wevertons. Sharp as lye and wickedly funny. A humor that truly bites. He doesn't talk much, except to Fairlie and me. He sees way too much and has a way of never forgetting. He knows how to hold a grudge. He's a majicar. I thought he was arrogant before—you know, being a Weverton, and even a minor one and his entire sense of privilege. But he's worse as a majicar. Has a way of looking down his nose, not that we let him get away with it much.

YOU CAN CLEARLY GET A LOT OF CHARACTER information using other characters' perceptions of them. In this case,

Ryland is talking about one of his best friends (majicar is a kind of wizard in this world). My goal in this interview was to get better acquainted with my characters and their voices as I was struggling to nail their voices in the novel (*The Turning Tide* in my Crosspointe series). This interview helped with that, but it gave me a great deal of insight into the three characters as well.

In this case, it's a very direct way of describing the other characters and gives you a strong sense of who they are, even in just a short paragraph. In the context of writing fiction, you don't often have the opportunity to have one character talk about other characters. What you do have are their impressions as their interactions go on. It might come in dialog:

"Do you always have to be an ass? From the day I met you, you've harped on me dressing better so you don't have to be embarrassed."

From that small quote, you know that whoever 'you' is, they dress well and likely like nice things. They probably drive a nice car and their home is designed to be admired. They also are self-important and require their companions to appear more elegant or wealthy so they they don't have to be embarrassed by being seen together. They also think they have a right or obligation to tell their companion to change to better suit their own sense of value.

The Take Away

CHARACTERS *ARE* THEIR PERCEPTIONS and their responses to those perceptions. Likewise, they are what other people notice about them. It's a powerful two-for-one tool because what Jane notices about Rodney not only tells readers what

Rodney's like, it gives insight into Jane. And finally, remember also that people have a tendency to notice what's on their mind. Pregnant women suddenly notice other pregnant women everywhere they go and never saw before. You can turn the inner life outward and reveal a lot through perception.

7

Habits, Rituals, and Doing the Things

HAVE you ever been doing something and somebody else comes over and tells you you're doing it wrong, and here's the right way? Or maybe you're the person watching someone else do the thing the wrong way, and it bugs you so much you have to go make them do it right.

I had a friend who's wife refused to let him mow the lawn because he'd leave little strands of long grass here and again. She hated it, hated that he wouldn't do it right, and so she took charge. And no, I don't know why she didn't let him do it and then go fix it, as that seems easier, and I also don't know why she wasn't just glad somebody else was doing it.

The point is that people have ways of doing things that they don't change. Some of those things approach the level of ritual, in that they are repeated the same way and in the same order. (You are now going to hear me repeat the word ritual far more times than you want, but bear with me. It's worth it). For instance: the bedtime ritual. That might mean putting on pajamas, washing your face, putting on moisturizer, brushing your teeth, combing your hair, reading a book, watching the news, or any number of other elements, all done in a particular order and in a particular way and at a particular time.

Rituals can circle around health routines, personality quirks, superstitions, ingrained habits, all of the above and more. What makes them interesting for character building is that these rituals are important to the characters and help them make sense of how the world works, or how they fit into it.

Think about how your character does repetitive tasks. How have they ritualized them? What happens if they cannot do that particular ritual? In an extreme case, your character might be a serial killer who likes to do his killing in a particular way and with particular tools. It might refer to a neurodivergent person who organizes his life around specific rituals. It might be someone who's created rituals to feel connected and centered.

Every ritual is individual and created from specific needs. You can look at your character and decide what ritual they might have, or you might come up with a ritual and figure out why they do it and what happens when they can't.

Not all habits and methods of doing things rise to the level of ritualistic behavior. However, identifying habits and methods for situations will give you a lot of meat to work with when establishing character. Some people establish necessary habits and then continue with them after the necessity has gone. For instance, when I was a kid and I wanted to ride a horse, I took a handful of oats and stood in the horse trough until my horse approached, then fed him the oats while sliding the reins around his neck. I'd then put the bridle on, lead him out, and brush him, and check his hooves, then take him to a stack of railroad ties and climb on.

I was short. It was necessary to get in the trough and to use the railroad ties. However I continued those habits long past when they were necessary because I stopped thinking about why I was doing them.

Your character might wash all their dishes by hand even though they have a dishwasher, because they got so used to not having a dishwasher that they don't think about using it. You might have someone who never spices their food, because for the longest time they cooked meals for people who didn't even like salt, much less cumin. Now that they can use spices, they are in the habit of going without. Or have been a foster kid and hoard food and belongings. Any of those tells you a lot about their backstory as well as their current thinking process.

Another character might call them out on their behavior, or note it as strange, which helps the reader focus on the how those behaviors define the character.

I love using habits and calling attention to them because they can really make a character unique and interesting. In *My Big Fat Greek Wedding*, the father liked to solve all the problems with Windex.

I've been watching *Death in Paradise*, a TV show set in the Caribbean, where it is hot and humid, yet the British detective wears a three piece suit and despite his discomfort, will not wear the lighter-weight local clothing. His identity is wrapped up in his suits, and to change would alter who he is in ways he's not prepared to deal with. So he suffers.

The Take Away

MAKE USE OF BEHAVIOR PATTERNS that involve personal rituals and habits when it comes to ordinary behavior. These are opportunities to establish character with ongoing behaviors, and they offer potentials for tension and conflict when other characters notice and/or call them out.

8

Likes, Dislikes, and Pet Peeves

Do people do things that just drive you up a wall? Maybe they snap their gum. Or mispronounce a word. Or use the wrong word. Or tap their legs all the time. Or always show up late? Or never follow through on a promise?

When you think about all the things in the world that can annoy people, you start to realize what a fertile concept this is for establishing character. I roll 'likes' into this category because some people's likes can be other's pet peeves. I might love incense and burn it round the clock. You might despise the stuff and would rather rip out your lungs than subject them to incense.

Someone might adore toy trains and building all the houses and tracks and scenery that goes with them, while another person finds that childish and boring and ridiculous. People who stop in the middle of the road until they can change lanes make me slightly murderous and don't even get me started on people who clog up the drive-through because they can't decide what to order.

The point I'm getting at is that likes, dislikes, and pet peeves all fit under the same preference umbrella, and because they are very personal, this category offers very fertile ground for character development.

There are multiple facets to how you might use preferences to establish character. Your character may despise liars. They might have a soft spot for children, or they may do everything in their power to avoid being around children and possibly call them crotch-goblins (indicating their level of disdain). A person might despise people who wear leather. Or people who constantly complain and refuse to try to fix the problem. Maybe they hate listening to Michael Jackson. Maybe they love wearing entire bottles of perfume.

A character's preferences give insight into who they are on a surface level. You can say Alex hates when people let their dogs into his yard. The surface interpretation offers several options as to what that might tell you about him. Maybe he hates dogs. Maybe the neighbors don't pick up after their dogs. Maybe the dogs chase his cats or dig holes. The context you've provided in the story will shed light on how a reader should interpret that bit of information.

However, you have the opportunity to deepen that understanding by giving backstory and offer insight about Alex's hatred of people who let their dogs into his yard. It's possible he grows dangerous-to-animals plants and doesn't want any dogs to get sick as happened to another dog when he was a child. His goal is to protect the dogs. That is an unexpected explanation and tells you Alex is thoughtful, likes animals, is responsible, and cares about the people who live around him. That's a lot to pack into one little pet peeve.

You can push on this particular trait throughout a novel, even attaching thematic ribbons to it, and use it to show a character's growth and change. You see this fairly frequently in curmudgeonly characters who slowly open up, and other characters realize that their peevishness (or pet-peevishness) is a way to control bits of their lives because the rest is so out of control. Like the hyper-clean fanatic, who is hiding the fact that he is an addict, and his personal life is a complete mess. By him learning to relax and be less of a clean-freak, he also demonstrates a willingness to show his uglier and messier addict side and possibly reach out for help.

You can have a neighbor character who hangs up dozens of wind chimes, because she claims your dogs bark so loudly, and she needs something to cover the sound. Only later you discover her own dog died, and it's painful for her to hear your dogs and be reminded of her own loss. Thematically, if you're writing about loss or getting over or past trauma, this pet peeve gives you an opportunity to offer a facet of how loss can stunt a person or how grieving can be misunderstood.

There is an amazing book called *The Things They Carried* by Tim O'Brien, about fighting in the Vietnam War. The titular first chapter talks about the various things that each man carries. These are definitional items for the characters because each also is carrying a heavy pack with required gear. Everything extra they carry has to be special and meaningful to that person because it adds weight to an already exhaustingly heavy burden. Some carry letters or pictures. Some carry drugs. Some carry a Bible. They all also carry intangibles. These are memories, fears, doubts, hopes, dreams…

Each of these items reflect a like, a dislike, or a pet peeve. More than that, these also are indicators of who these men are, and each of these things bears more story weight than a mere preference, because these things are tied to themes and to the overall character arcs.

If you choose preferences wisely and showcase them in the context of your characters and themes, you'll find that they add depth and intricacy to your story in ways that are difficult to do otherwise.

The Take Away

BE AWARE OF AND CAREFULLY use preferences in your novel. It's easy to overlook their potential and think they are just fun ways to establish character, but these likes, dislikes, and pet-peeves often come from deep within a person and establish a pathway to seeing inside their subconscious and their true fears and feelings.

9

Choices and Secrets

THIS IS POSSIBLY the most simple and yet most useful tool you have for establishing and developing a character. The choices they make underpin many of the previous character elements. Choices reveal more than anything else about a character.

We've talked a little about preferences, which will then result in choices, so you can work backward from choices to understand likes, dislikes, and pet-peeves. Like I said, it's simple. You can also look at backstory and predict a character's choices, and backward engineer the backstory based on choices that they've made. Again, simple.

Remember that when I say simple, I mean the concept makes sense. Doing it might not be easy, but you understand what the process is and how it works.

What I want to call your attention to, however, is a particular kind of choice. Choosing what to have for dinner or what movie to watch or what to wear is pretty basic and nothing worth discussing here, because I'm sure you've got plenty of ideas for how your characters will decide.

What is worth discussing is choice of action. You've heard the phrase 'actions speak louder than words,' or 'watch what they say, not what they do,' because what they do is the truth. (Unless it's not because you're a twisty author).

What people do reveals everything about who they are, especially when nobody is looking. As a writer, you are always looking at your characters, and so is the reader, but you create the atmosphere of that character acting without consequence because nobody in the character's world is watching. That lack of consequence or judgement is critical because when they aren't watched, people can do unexpected things.

Laws, social morés, social expectations, peer pressure... all these external things will push people to act properly while under observation. Remove those guide rails and give them freedom to break the rules without repercussion. Make sure they won't be judged by friends, strangers, or the law. What will they do when they are free to do anything? Giving your characters that opportunity to act on choices in secret circumstances will reveal who they are in a raw way that you might not otherwise be able to do.

Another fertile element of character choice revolves around possibility. Every time someone makes a choice, they choose a path. It's a path that forks over and over and over with every subsequent choice the character makes. There are infinite paths and infinite possibilities. Every choice closes off some options and opens up others. The key as a writer is to choose the possibilities that tell your readers the most about your character.

That idea—that action reveals character—shouldn't be a surprise. In fact, you might be saying, *no, duh, Diana*. After all, stories by definition are driven by characters making choices and dealing with conflicts. In this case, I want you to consider one facet of that truth in a little more detail.

The choices every character makes both defines a character and also is a result of what you already know about them. If you're at the beginning of the writing process, then you might not know enough about your character to predict his choices, which means that you have an opportunity to play and grow your character in new ways. Start by throwing in unexpected choices.

For instance, make a list of ten things your character could do in response to being told they are going to be given a house for free. What if their choice is to create a safe space for old hens when they no longer lay eggs? Or possibly turn it into a halfway house for were-rats? Or sell it to fund a bucket-list trip to Hoboken, New Jersey? (If you don't, you should have all kinds of questions about why Hoboken is a bucket-list trip).

Anytime your character makes a choice, you have the opportunity to do something unexpected that allows you to reveal something new about them or deepen the characterization. In particular, if you seem to go against who they are and then show the action is totally within their character, you can give your reader a little reader-gasm. Those moments are exciting and unexpected and make a reader want to keep turning pages to see what else you have up your sleeve.

How a character handles a situation is also an important characterization tool. Some people pause and think how to best respond in a situation. Others just shoot from the hip and react on sheer instinct. Some people make a decision to react a particular way based on logic. Others take a moment and then go with the more emotional reaction.

For instance, Sam is about to go into a party to celebrate his anniversary with his husband, Mark, but just as he steps inside, he finds out Mark has a whole other family.

In your novel, this is a pinch point, so a lot will hinge on how he handles the situation. His major options are to:

1. RESPOND ON INSTINCT AND WALK OUT, get into a fight on the spot, withdraw emotionally and let things happen around him, and a host of other things. The point is that he doesn't think and responds reflexively.

2. THINK OF HIS OPTIONS AND CHOOSE ONE. Maybe the world slows down, and he thinks a whole lot of things in the space of an instant but manages to make a decision on how to act. All of the above actions are on the table, but this time he's considered what might be best for him and does it.

EITHER OPTION IS VALID AND VALUABLE, but one is a response to instinct, the other involves careful thought. What a person does on instinct might be the exact opposite of what he'd do after he has a chance to think. Imagine a character who responds reflexively with hurt and anger. On the other hand, give that same character a moment to think, and he becomes manipulative and uses the moment for blackmail.

The Take Away

AS WRITERS, WE TEND TO THINK OF CHOICES and methods of handling a situation as plot points, which they are. Plot, by definition, is a causal sequence of events. There is a causal link between events. Basically, it means that because X happened, Y then happened, which then caused Z. The cause that drives plotting comes from the characters and their choices and their methods of handling of situations. Stuff doesn't just happen. It happens because a character made it happen that way. Seize these moments to deepen and round out your character.

10

One Last thing

I WANTED to give you one last important thing to think about: *dramatic irony*.

Dramatic irony is when the reader knows more than the character. It might be that the reader is aware of events happening that the character isn't. Or it might be that the reader knows how other people feel, and the character is in the dark.

Readers ***ADORE*** dramatic irony. (They must because it's all-capped, italicized, and bolded it, so take heed). There is a deliciousness that comes from that feeling of being in the know and anticipating the moment when the character finds out. We see this often in romance novels when the reader is given access to the thoughts of the lovers, and yet the lovers are oblivious to what the other is thinking.

Likewise, when you know what bad things are coming, and the hero is blissfully unaware, you become almost giddy with fear for them. At the same time, anticipation for what they'll do thrills you and you begin to obsess over how they'll handle it and what they'll have to sacrifice.

I wanted to leave you with this concept because I believe that if you can nail dramatic irony, you'll achieve passionate fans.

Now go forth and write. I hope that this little book has given you some tools to help you build engaging characters that readers will love and hate.

Do feel free to go to my website, and let me know how this book has impacted you. I would love to hear.

Come visit me at www.dianapfrancis.com or send me an email at dpf@dianapfrancis.com.

About Diana Pharaoh Francis

Diana Pharaoh Francis is the USA Today and Amazon Bestselling writer of fantastical, adventurous, and often romantic fiction. She holds a Ph.D. in Victorian literature and literary theory. She's owned by a corgi, a mini blue heeler, and a blue-eyed corgi mix. She spends much of her time gardening, airbrush painting, herding children, and avoiding housework. She likes rocks, geocaching, horses, knotting up yarn, and has a thing for 1800s England, especially the Victorians.

For more about her books and to sign up for her newsletter, visit her website: www.dianapfrancis.com

Acknowledgements

Acknowledgements

This book has grown out of a vast number of experiences teaching students, talking to writers, conference presentations, teaching workshops, critiquing, and trying to solve my own character conundrums. I have to start by saying that every book I've ever read, every writing conversation, every interaction with words and characters and stories has allowed me to write this book and I thank the universe giving me the creativity and the playground for making stories, and readers for reading them.

I also want to thank my patrons on Patreon, especially Barb Cass, the members of BVC for their input and aid, especially Pat Rice and Jennifer Stevenson. Lyn Forester made an amazing cover, and thanks to all my readers who helped me decide on the cover.

Thank you to Devon Monk, as always something of a muse, an emotional support writer, and general cheerleader. Thanks also to Christy Keyes, Melissa Marr, Barb Hendee, and Melissa Sawmiller for giving me feedback.

Acknowledgements

Thanks to my family who is always there to keep me going, and thanks to my three hooligan dogs to keep me laughing and snuggling and warm.

About Book View Café

Book View Café is a professional authors' published cooperative offering DRM-free e-books in multiple formats to readers around the world. With authors in a variety of genres, including mystery, romance, fantasy, and science fiction. The Café has something for everyone.

BVC is good for readers because you can enjoy high-quality DRM-free ebooks from your favorite authors at a reasonable price. Book View Café is good for writers because 90% of the proceeds goes directly to the book's author.

Our authors include New York Times and USA Today bestsellers, Nebula, Hugo, Lambda, Chanticleer, National Reader's Choice, and Philip K. Dick Award Winners, World Fantasy, Kirkus, and Rita Award nominees, and winners and nominees of many other publishing awards.

BVC's newsletter includes new releases, specials, author news, and event announcements. Click here to sign up.

BOOK VIEW CAFE

To My Readers

Thank you for hanging out with me! I hope this book is useful for you. If you enjoyed *The Quick and Dirty Guide to Character Building*, consider leaving a review on your favorite book-buying site and telling your friends. Also, read excerpts from my other books on my website and sign up for my newsletter to hear more about upcoming releases at: www.-dianapfrancis.com

www.ingramcontent.com/pod-product-compliance
Lightning Source LLC
Chambersburg PA
CBHW061804070526
44586CB00023B/2709